MEGA MACHINES

FIRST EDITION
DK LONDON: Series Editor Deborah Lock; **US Senior Editor** Shannon Beatty;
Project Art Editor Hoa Luc; **Producer, Pre-Production** Francesca Wardell; **Illustrator** Hoa Luc;
Reading Consultant Linda Gambrell, PhD; **DK DELHI: Editor** Pomona Zaheer;
Assistant Art Editor Yamini Panwar; **DTP Designers** Anita Yadav, Syed Md Farhan;
Picture Researcher Sumedha Chopra; **Deputy Managing Editor** Soma Chowdhury

THIS EDITION
Editorial Management by Oriel Square
Produced for DK by WonderLab Group LLC
Jennifer Emmett, Erica Green, Kate Hale, *Founders*

Editors Grace Hill Smith, Libby Romero, Maya Myers, Michaela Weglinski;
Photography Editors Kelley Miller, Annette Kiesow, Nicole DiMella;
Managing Editor Rachel Houghton; **Designers** Project Design Company;
Researcher Michelle Harris; **Copy Editor** Lori Merritt; **Indexer** Connie Binder;
Proofreader Larry Shea; **Reading Specialist** Dr. Jennifer Albro; **Curriculum Specialist** Elaine Larson

The publisher would like to thank the following for their kind permission to reproduce their images:
a=above; c=center; b=below; l=left; r=right; t=top; b/g=background

123RF.com: nerthuz 3cb; **Dreamstime.com:** Marko Bukorovic 20-21b, Oleg Doroshin 8bl, Joseph Gough 22b, 30cla, Bogdan Hoda 23b, Grigorii Ialukov 8-9bc, 11bl, Dmitry Kalinovsky 4-5, 29b, Chinnasorn Pangcharoen 14-15b, Photovs 16bc, 30tl, Oleksandr Rado 26-27b, Maksim Safaniuk 12-13b, Thaweesak Thipphamon 25bl, Eduard Zayonchkovski 19c, Hongqi Zhang (aka Michael Zhang) 6b, 20c, 30bl; **Getty Images / iStock:** E+ / kali9 28b; **Shutterstock.com:** Double_H 24b

Cover images: *Front:* **Dreamstime.com:** Bluezace (Trucks), Zbynek Burival (Background);
Back: **Dreamstime.com:** Onyxprj cla, cra

All other images © Dorling Kindersley
For more information see: www.dkimages.com

For the curious
www.dk.com

MEGA MACHINES

Deborah Lock

Contents

Stage 1: Clearing the Site

"Hard hats on!" says the supervisor, getting to work.
"Welcome to the construction site.

supervisor

The plans are ready for building a new school. The mega machines are ready to start work."

plans

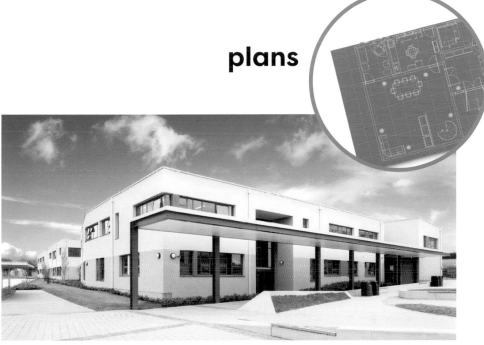

This is what the new school will look like.

"Here they come!"

Rumble, rumble!

The site is not level, and it is covered with rubble.
"What a mess!" says the supervisor, scratching his head.
"We need the bulldozer, front loader, and dump truck!" he says.
The bulldozer pushes the dirt and rubble with its blade.

tracks

It moves forward slowly.

Hum, rumble, hum!

bulldozer

blade

The front loader scoops
up the mounds of dirt
and rubble.
The bucket moves.

Forward ... down ...
scoop ... up!

The front loader
will carry its loaded
bucket up high.

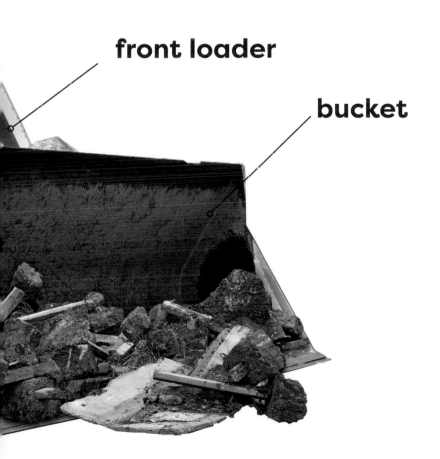

front loader

bucket

The dump truck will take the dirt and rubble away. The bucket of the front loader tips its load into the dumping bed.

Swish, clatter, clatter, swish!

The front loader
goes back and forth
to collect some more.
"Stage 1 is done," says
the supervisor, nodding
his head.

Stage 2: Digging the Site

"What a noise!" shouts the supervisor, covering his ears.
The site is now clear, and the excavator has arrived.

excavator

The excavator can dig deep holes. The arm moves up, out, and down.

Lower ... scoop ... lift ... turn ... drop ... turn!

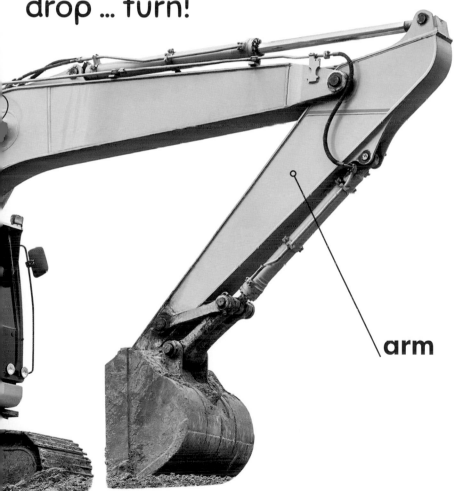

arm

Whirr, rumble, whirr!

Along comes the
concrete mixer.
The mixing drum
must keep spinning.
"Pour the concrete
into the hole," orders
the supervisor.
"Leave it to harden."

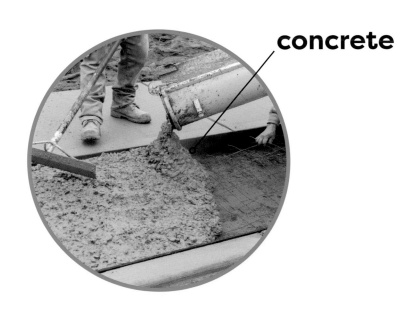

concrete

More holes are dug
and filled.
This makes a firm base
for the new school.

mixing drum

**concrete
mixer**

The holes have been filled.
The concrete is hard.
Here comes the roller to make the ground smooth and flat.

Roll, press, smooth!

The roller squashes down the dirt.
"Stage 2 is done," says the supervisor.

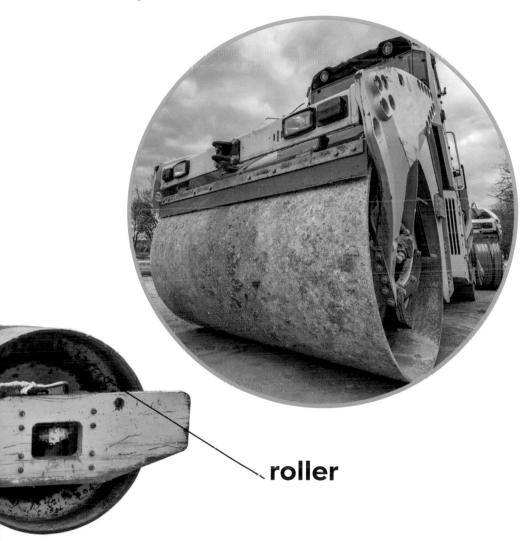

roller

Stage 3: Building the Frame

"Raise the crane," the supervisor tells the driver.

mobile crane

Up, up goes the boom of the mobile crane. The hook hangs from the chain at the end of the boom.

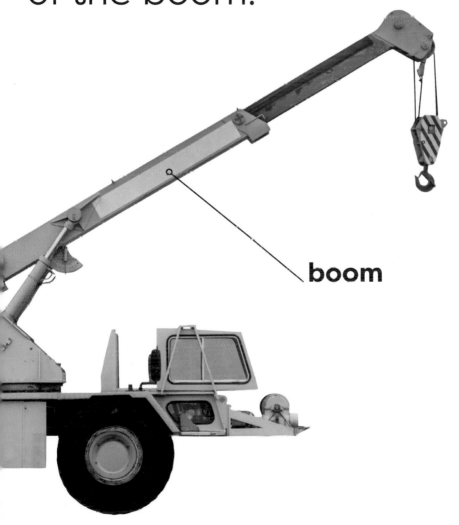

boom

The long trucks bring the strong steel girders. The crane driver moves the levers to lower the hook.

Lower ... hook ... lift ... turn ... lower ... fit ... unhook!

girder

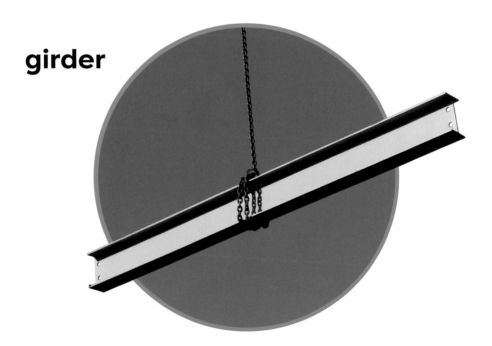

The hook picks the girders up one by one.

hook

The girders are
fitted together.
The crane swings back
and forth.

The girders will support the floors and the roof of the school.
The workers bolt the girders together.

Turn, twist, tighten!

"Stage 3 is done," says the supervisor.
He gives a thumbs-up.

Stage 4: Finishing the School

"One month left," the supervisor tells the crew. The huge trucks arrive with their heavy loads.

There are bricks and white siding. There are shiny windows and tall doors. The bricklayers spread the mortar and lay the bricks.

siding

"One week left.
Let's work together!"
shouts the supervisor,
checking the plans.
The delivery trucks arrive.
Everyone helps to unload
the furniture and carry it
all into the school.

"Stage 4 is done.
Good job!" says
the supervisor.
The new school
is finished.
The mega machines
rumble away.

Rumble, hum, rumble!

Glossary

concrete
a mix of cement, sand, small stones, and water

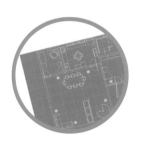

girder
a steel beam used for the frame of a building

plans
drawings that show how to make a building or object

siding
a layer that protects the outside of a building

supervisor
a person in charge of workers

Index

Quiz

Answer the questions to see what you have learned. Check your answers with an adult.

1. Which vehicles are used to clear rubble and level the site?

2. What is the excavator used for?

3. What does the roller do?

4. Which parts of the crane work together to lift heavy objects?

5. What will support the floors and the roof of the school?

1. The bulldozer, the front loader, and the dump truck
2. Digging deep holes 3. It makes the ground smooth and flat
4. The boom, the chain, and the hook 5. The girders